EXPLORING LIFE CYCLES

Plants

Aaron Carr

AV2

www.av2books.com

Step 1
Go to **www.av2books.com**

Step 2
Enter this unique code

DECASQIKW

Step 3
Explore your interactive eBook!

EXPLORING
LIFE
CYCLES

Plants

AV2

Start!

AV2 is optimized for use on any device

Your interactive
eBook comes with...

Read

Audio
Listen to the entire
book read aloud

Videos
Watch informative
video clips

Weblinks
Gain additional
information for research

Try This!
Complete activities and
hands-on experiments

Key Words
Study vocabulary, and
complete a matching
word activity

Quizzes
Test your knowledge

Slideshows
View images and captions

View new titles and product videos at
www.av2books.com

EXPLORING LIFE CYCLES

Plants

CONTENTS

3

All plants begin life, grow, and make more plants.

This is a life cycle.

Plants begin life as seeds.

Seeds need plenty of water. This helps them grow into healthy plants.

When a seed sprouts,
it is called a seedling.

Some seeds sprout and begin to grow after one week. Others may take months to sprout.

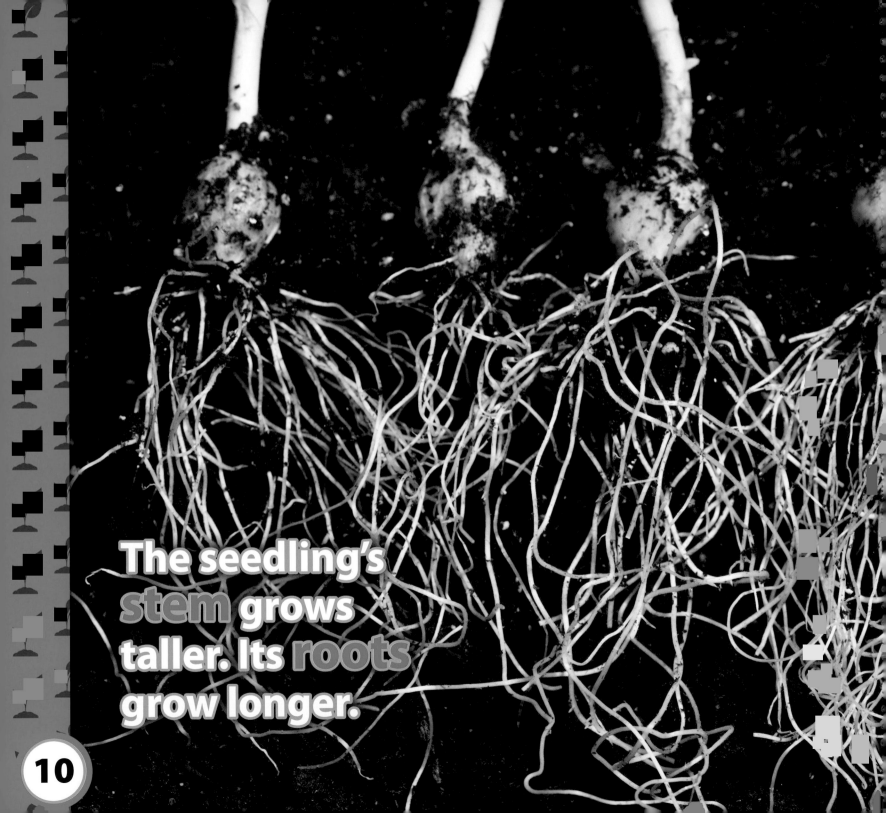

The seedling's stem grows taller. Its roots grow longer.

Leaves start to grow from the stem.

Over time, the seedling becomes a fully grown plant.

Most plants have flowers.

Plants use sunlight to make their food. They need the Sun to live.

The more sunlight a plant gets, the bigger it can grow.

Flowers make seeds. Plants **spread** the seeds to make new plants.

Some plants use the wind to spread their seeds.

Then, the life cycle begins again.

18

Some plants finish their life cycle in one year. Others take many years.

Plants come in different sizes, colors, and shapes.

The way a plant looks is passed on through its seeds.

A seed from a tulip will grow into another tulip.

Life Cycles Quiz

A plant's life cycle has three stages.

Which stage of the life cycle do you see in each picture?

Plant

Seed

Seedling

23

KEY WORDS

Research has shown that as much as 65 percent of all written material published in English is made up of 300 words. These 300 words cannot be taught using pictures or learned by sounding them out. They must be recognized by sight. This book contains 56 common sight words to help young readers improve their reading fluency and comprehension. This book also teaches young readers several important content words, such as proper nouns. These words are paired with pictures to aid in learning and improve understanding.

Page	Sight Words First Appearance	Page	Content Words First Appearance
4	a, all, and, grow, is, life, make, more, plants, this	4	life cycle
6	as	6	seeds
7	helps, into, need, of, them, water	8	seedling
8	it, when	9	months, week
9	after, may, one, others, some, take, to	10	roots, stem
10	its, the	13	flowers
11	from, leaves, start	14	Sun, sunlight
12	over, time	17	wind
13	have, most	20	colors, shapes, sizes
14	food, live, their, they, use	21	tulip
15	can, gets		
16	new		
17	again, then		
19	in, many, year		
20	come, different		
21	another, looks, on, through, way, will		

Published by AV2
350 5th Avenue, 59th Floor New York, NY 10118
Website: www.av2books.com

Library of Congress Cataloging-in-Publication Data
Names: Carr, Aaron, author.
Title: Plants / Aaron Carr.
Description: New York, NY : AV2, [2021] | Series: Exploring life cycles | Audience: Ages 4-8 | Audience: Grades K-1
Identifiers: LCCN 2020011801 (print) | LCCN 2020011802 (ebook) | ISBN 9781791127244 (library binding) | ISBN 9781791127251 (paperback) | ISBN 9781791127268 | ISBN 9781791127275
Subjects: LCSH: Plants--Juvenile literature.
Classification: LCC QK49 .C337 2021 (print) | LCC QK49 (ebook) | DDC 580--dc23
LC record available at https://lccn.loc.gov/2020011801
LC ebook record available at https://lccn.loc.gov/2020011802

Printed in Guangzhou, China
1 2 3 4 5 6 7 8 9 0 24 23 22 21 20

042020
100919

Art Director: Terry Paulhus Project Coordinator: John Willis

Every reasonable effort has been made to trace ownership and to obtain permission to reprint copyright material. The publisher would be pleased to have any errors or omissions brought to its attention so that they may be corrected in subsequent printings.

The publisher acknowledges Getty Images and iStock as the primary image suppliers for this title.